COOL
Hamburger
Recipes

Main Dishes for Beginning Chefs

Alex Kuskowski

**Checkerboard
Library**

An Imprint of Abdo Publishing
abdopublishing.com

abdopublishing.com

Published by Abdo Publishing, a division of ABDO, PO Box 398166, Minneapolis, Minnesota 55439. Copyright © 2017 by Abdo Consulting Group, Inc. International copyrights reserved in all countries. No part of this book may be reproduced in any form without written permission from the publisher. Checkerboard Library™ is a trademark and logo of Abdo Publishing.

Printed in the United States of America,
North Mankato, Minnesota
102016
012017

Design and Production: Mighty Media, Inc.
Series Editor: Liz Salzmann
Photo Credits: Mighty Media, Inc.; Shutterstock

The following manufacturers/names appearing in this book are trademarks: Essential Everyday™, Lea & Perrins®, Oster®, Pyrex®

Publisher's Cataloging-in-Publication Data

Names: Kuskowski, Alex, author.
Title: Cool hamburger recipes: main dishes for beginning chefs / by Alex Kuskowski.
Other titles: Main dishes for beginning chefs
Description: Minneapolis, MN : Abdo Publishing, 2017. | Series: Cool main dish recipes | Includes bibliographical references and index.
Identifiers: LCCN 2016944832 | ISBN 9781680781359 (lib. bdg.) | ISBN 9781680775556 (ebook)
Subjects: LCSH: Cooking--Juvenile literature. | Dinners and dining--Juvenile literature. | Entrees (Cooking)--Juvenile literature. | One-dish meals--Juvenile literature.
Classification: DDC 641.82--dc23
LC record available at http://lccn.loc.gov/2016944832

TO ADULT HELPERS

Get cooking! This is your chance to help a budding chef. Being able to cook meals is a life skill. Learning to cook gives kids new experiences and helps them gain confidence. These recipes are designed to help kids learn how to cook on their own. They may need more assistance on some recipes than others. Be there to offer guidance when they need it. Encourage them to do as much as they can on their own. Make sure to have rules for cleanup. There should always be adult supervision when kids are using sharp utensils or a hot oven or stove.

SAFETY FIRST!

Some recipes call for activities that require caution. If you see these symbols, ask an adult for help.

HOT STUFF!

This recipe requires the use of a stove or oven. Always use pot holders when handling hot objects.

SUPER SHARP!

This recipe includes the use of a sharp utensil, such as a knife or grater.

Contents

Hooray for Hamburger!

The main dish is where you start when planning a meal. It's the most important part. Then you choose salads, side dishes, and **desserts** to go with the main dish. Hamburger is a great base for many main dishes. It is a favorite meat of people all over the world. It's easy to make, tasty to eat, and there are tons of ways to prepare it!

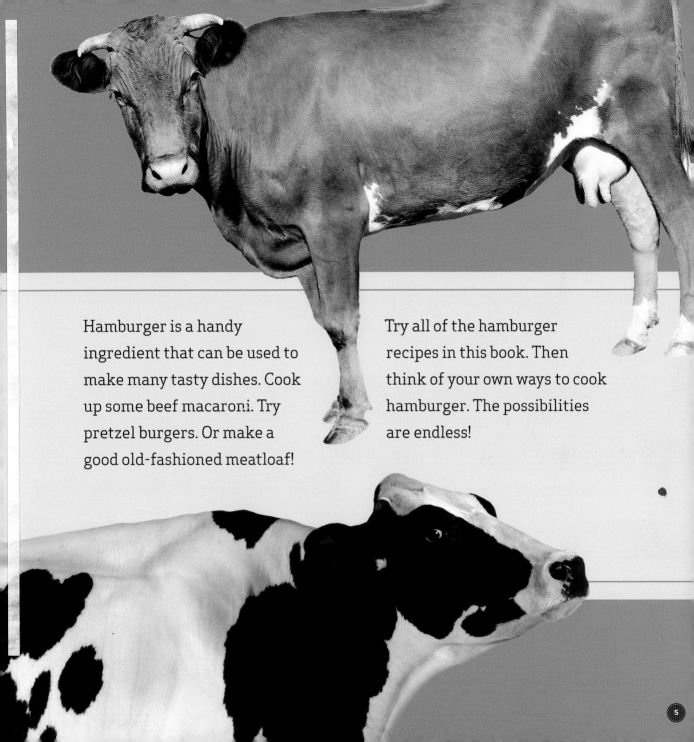

Hamburger is a handy ingredient that can be used to make many tasty dishes. Cook up some beef macaroni. Try pretzel burgers. Or make a good old-fashioned meatloaf!

Try all of the hamburger recipes in this book. Then think of your own ways to cook hamburger. The possibilities are endless!

I ♥ HAMBURGER

Hamburger meat has many names. Ground beef. Beef mince. Minced meat. It is cow meat cut up into small pieces. It is used to make some of the most popular foods ever, including hamburgers!

PICKING THE MEAT

If you can, get fresh ground meat. Check the amount of fat in the meat. It will be listed on the outside of the package. Pick ground meat with a low fat content.

KEEP IT CLEAN

Wash your hands before and after touching the meat. Wash any **utensils** that touched raw meat separately from other dishes.

COOKING THE MEAT

Heat the pan or grill before cooking. Make sure it is hot. Then add the meat. Cook over medium heat. Cook the meat until there is no pink left. Pink meat is still uncooked. But don't cook it too long, either. Overcooking makes the meat dry.

COOKING BASICS

Ask Permission

- Before you cook, ask **permission** to use the kitchen, cooking tools, and ingredients.

- If you'd like to do something yourself, say so! Just remember to be safe.

- If you would like help, ask for it!

Be Prepared

- Be organized. Knowing where everything is makes cooking safer and more fun!

- Read the directions all the way through before starting a recipe. Follow the directions in order.

- The most important ingredient is preparation! Make sure you have everything you'll need.

Be Smart, Be Safe

- Never cook if you are home alone.

- Always have an adult nearby for hot jobs, such as using the oven or the stove.

- Have an adult around when using a sharp tool, such as a knife or a grater. Always be careful when using these tools!

- Remember to turn pot handles toward the back of the stove. That way you won't accidentally knock the pots over.

Be Neat, Be Clean

- Start with clean hands, clean tools, and a clean work surface.

- Tie back long hair to keep it out of the food.

- Wear comfortable clothing and roll up your sleeves.

- Put extra ingredients and tools away when you're done.

- Wash all the dishes and **utensils**. Clean up your workspace.

COOKING TERMS

BOIL

Boil means to heat liquid until it begins to bubble.

DICE

Dice means to cut something into small squares.

DRAIN

Drain means to remove liquid using a colander or the pot lid.

SHRED

Shred means to cut small pieces of something using a grater.

SLICE

Slice means to cut something into pieces of the same thickness.

CHOP

Chop means to cut something into small pieces.

CRUSH

Crush means to break something into **crumbs** with a rolling pin.

GREASE

Grease means to coat something with butter or cooking spray.

MINCE

Mince means to cut or chop something into very tiny pieces.

SPREAD

Spread means to make a smooth layer with a spoon, knife, or spatula.

STIR

Stir means to mix ingredients together, usually with a large spoon.

INGREDIENTS

Here are some of the ingredients you will need.

9-inch pie crust

brown sugar

eggs

elbow macaroni

garlic

green cabbage

milk

mozzarella cheese

mustard

onion

Ritz crackers

spaghetti sauce

thyme

tomato paste

12

carrots

cheddar cheese

chili powder

condensed tomato soup

ground beef

ground cumin

hamburger buns

ketchup

parsley

potato

pretzel twists

refrigerated biscuits

tomato sauce

vegetable oil

white vinegar

Worcestershire sauce

13

TOOLS

Here are some of the tools you will need.

5 × 9-inch loaf pan

aluminum foil

cutting board

grill

large pot

mixing spoon

plastic zipper bags

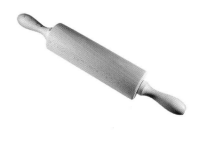

rolling pin

baking sheet

basting brush

colander

measuring cups

measuring spoons

mixing bowls

rubber spatula

sharp knife

spatula

SAVORY
Sloppy Joes

Make a messy meal that's tough to resist!

potato chips
1½ pounds ground beef
½ cup chopped onion
1 can condensed tomato
   soup
¼ cup ketchup
1 tablespoon white vinegar
¼ cup brown sugar

1 teaspoon Worcestershire
   sauce
8 hamburger buns

sharp knife
cutting board
measuring cups
measuring spoons
plastic zipper bag
rolling pin
large pot with lid
mixing spoon
pot holders

1. Fill a plastic bag with potato chips. Crush them with a rolling pin. Measure 1 cup of **crumbs**.

2. Put the ground beef in a large pot over medium heat. Stir and cook for 8 minutes, or until the meat is brown.

3. Stir in the onion. Cook for 5 minutes. Use the pot lid to drain the grease from the pan.

4. Turn the heat to low. Stir in the soup, ketchup, vinegar, sugar, Worcestershire sauce, and potato chip crumbs. Cook for 8 to 10 minutes.

5. Put some of the meat mixture on each hamburger bun.

3

4

5

MINI
Beefy Pizzas

Sink your teeth into tiny, meaty pizzas!

10 refrigerated biscuits
1 pound ground beef
½ cup chopped onion
1 garlic clove, minced
½ teaspoon salt
½ teaspoon black pepper
1½ cups spaghetti sauce

1 cup shredded mozzarella cheese

measuring cups
measuring spoons
sharp knife
cutting board
baking sheet
pot holders
large pot with lid
mixing spoon

1. Bake the biscuits according to the directions on the package. Let them cool.

2. Put the ground beef, onion, garlic, salt, and pepper in a large pot. Set the heat to medium. Stir and cook for 10 minutes or until the meat is brown. Use the pot lid to drain the extra liquid. Stir in the spaghetti sauce.

2

3. Preheat the oven to 400 degrees. Cut the biscuits in half. Lay them on the baking sheet with the inside facing up.

3

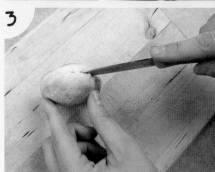

4. Put 1 tablespoon of the meat mixture on each biscuit half.

5. Sprinkle cheese on top of each one. Bake for 7 minutes.

4

HAMBURGER
Pocket Pies

1 tablespoon vegetable oil

1 pound ground beef

1 cup shredded green
cabbage

2 cups diced potatoes

1 carrot, sliced

3 tablespoons tomato paste

½ teaspoon
Worcestershire sauce

½ teaspoon thyme

2 9-inch pie crusts

measuring
spoons

measuring
cups

sharp knife

cutting board

baking sheet

aluminum foil

large pot
with lid

mixing spoon

basting brush

fork

pot holders

1 Preheat the oven to 400 degrees. Cover the baking sheet with foil. Put the oil in a large pot. Heat it over medium heat. Add the meat. Stir and cook for 7 minutes.

2 Add the cabbage, potatoes, and carrots. Stir and cook for 9 minutes. Stir in the tomato paste, Worcestershire sauce, and thyme. Cover the pot. Cook for 15 minutes.

3 Cut the pie crusts in half. Put ½ cup of the meat mixture on each half. Brush the edges of the crusts with water.

4 Fold the crust over the filling. Press the edges together with a fork. Make three small cuts in the top of each pie. Put the pies on the baking sheet. Bake for 20 minutes or until the edges of the crusts are golden brown.

2

3

4

Crunchy
Pretzel Burgers

This burger has a surprising crunch!

small pretzel twists
1 pound ground beef
1 egg
½ cup chopped onion
1 teaspoon black pepper
4 hamburger buns

measuring cups
sharp knife
cutting board
measuring spoons
baking sheet
aluminum foil

plastic zipper bag
rolling pin
mixing bowl
pot holders

1 Preheat the oven to 375 degrees. Cover the baking sheet with aluminum foil.

2 Fill the plastic bag with pretzels. Crush them with a rolling pin. Measure ¾ cup of **crumbs**.

3 Put the ground beef, pretzel crumbs, egg, onion, and pepper in a bowl. Mix with your hands.

4 Divide the mixture into four equal parts. Shape each part into a **patty**.

5 Put the patties on the baking sheet. Press a pretzel onto each patty.

6 Bake for 10 minutes. Serve the patties on hamburger buns.

3

4

5

BEST
Cheesy Burgers

There's melty cheese in every bite!

1¼ pounds ground beef
½ teaspoon garlic powder
1 teaspoon salt
1 teaspoon Worcestershire
  sauce
½ teaspoon black pepper
sliced cheddar cheese
4 hamburger buns

measuring spoons
mixing bowl
grill
spatula
pot holders

1. Put the meat, garlic powder, salt, Worcestershire sauce, and pepper in a large bowl. Mix with your hands.

2. Divide the meat into eight equal parts. Shape each part into a **patty**. Make them ¼ inch (0.6 cm) thick.

3. Put two small cheese slices between two patties. Pinch the edges of the patties together. Repeat with the remaining patties.

4. Heat the grill to medium-high. Place the patties on the grill. Cook for 4 minutes. Flip the patties. Cook for 3 more minutes. Do not press on the patties while they are cooking.

5. Take the patties off the grill. Let them cool for 5 minutes. Serve them on hamburger buns.

1

3

4

YUMMY
Classic Meatloaf

Make meatloaf as good as your mom's!

non-stick cooking spray
Ritz crackers
½ onion, chopped
2 tablespoons butter
2 teaspoons minced garlic
1½ pounds ground beef
1 egg
1 cup milk

2 tablespoons brown sugar
⅔ cup ketchup
1½ tablespoons mustard
1 tablespoon Worcestershire sauce
1 teaspoon salt
½ teaspoon black pepper

sharp knife
cutting board
measuring spoons
measuring cups
5 × 9-inch loaf pan
plastic zipper bag

rolling pin
saucepan
mixing spoon
mixing bowls
whisk
rubber spatula
pot holders

1 Preheat the oven to 350 degrees. Grease the loaf pan with cooking spray. Fill a plastic bag with crackers. Crush them with a rolling pin. Measure 1 cup of **crumbs**.

2 Put the onion, butter, and garlic in the saucepan. Cook over medium heat for 5 minutes. Take the pan off the heat.

3 Put the onion mixture, ground beef, egg, milk, and cracker crumbs in a large mixing bowl. Stir well. Spoon the mixture into the loaf pan.

4 Put the brown sugar, ketchup, mustard, Worcestershire sauce, salt, and pepper in a small mixing bowl. Whisk together. Spread the mixture on top of the meatloaf. Bake for 1 hour and 45 minutes.

2

3

4

BEEF & CHEESE Macaroni

8 ounces elbow macaroni
2 tablespoons olive oil
1 pound ground beef
1 cup chopped onion
½ teaspoon ground cumin
¼ teaspoon chili powder
¼ teaspoon salt
¼ teaspoon black pepper

2 8-ounce cans tomato sauce
¼ cup chopped parsley

measuring spoons
measuring cups
sharp knife
cutting board
large pot
colander
pot holders
mixing spoon

1 Cook the macaroni according to the directions on the package. Drain the macaroni with a colander.

2 Put the oil in a large pot. Heat it over medium heat. Add the ground beef and onion. Stir and cook for 5 minutes.

3 Stir in the cumin, chili powder, salt, and pepper.

4 Add the tomato sauce. Cook until it begins to boil. Turn off the heat. Stir in the macaroni and parsley.

1

2

4

Conclusion

Explore the world
of hamburger dishes.
What else can
you cook up?

Main dishes are fun to make and share! Feel proud of the dishes you prepare. Eat them with your family and friends. Hamburger meat is one of many great ingredients for main dishes. Don't stop with hamburger. Try other ingredients too!

Glossary

crumb – a tiny piece of something, especially food.

dessert – a sweet food, such as fruit, ice cream, or pastry, served after a meal.

patty – a round, flat cake made with chopped or ground food.

permission – when a person in charge says it's okay to do something.

utensil – a tool used to prepare or eat food.

WEBSITES

To learn more about Cool Main Dishes, visit **booklinks.abdopublishing.com**. These links are routinely monitored and updated to provide the most current information available.

Index